T0194989

HANDBOOK
for People Who Are Hurting

Learn to Cope with Hope

Mary A. Brown, M.Ed., D. Min.

WESTBOW
PRESS®
A DIVISION OF THOMAS NELSON
& ZONDERVAN

Scripture taken from the King James Version of the Holy Bible (Authorized Version of 1611). Public domain.

Scripture taken from THE HOLY BIBLE, NEW INTERNATIONAL VERSION®, NIV® Copyright © 1973, 1978, 1984, 2011 by Biblica, Inc.® Used by permission. All rights reserved worldwide.

Scripture taken from the NEW AMERICAN STANDARD BIBLE®, Copyright © 1960, 1962, 1963, 1968, 1971, 1972, 1973, 1975, 1977, 1995 by The Lockman Foundation. Used by permission.

WestBow Press books may be ordered through booksellers or by contacting:

WestBow Press
A Division of Thomas Nelson & Zondervan
1663 Liberty Drive
Bloomington, IN 47403
www.westbowpress.com
1 (866) 928-1240

ISBN: 978-1-9736-3745-5 (sc)
ISBN: 978-1-9736-3747-9 (hc)
ISBN: 978-1-9736-3746-2 (e)

Library of Congress Control Number: 2018910015

Print information available on the last page.

WestBow Press rev. date: 08/29/2018

Contents

Acknowledgement

To God be the Glory!

Introduction

This Handbook is a simple guide for people who are hurting and have a desire to overcome their hurts and pain *God's way.*

Individuals are expected to learn how to *cope* with *hope* as they discover and understand their *God-given* purpose for life.

People who are hurting are encouraged to establish a relationship with God and develop a basic foundation of biblical knowledge, prayer and fasting, praise and worship, salvation, and the Holy Spirit.

Unless otherwise noted, all biblical references in this book are taken from the King James Version of the Bible.

Cope

To deal effectively with something difficult.
To face and deal with responsibilities, problems or difficult
situations successfully or in a calm or adequate manner.
-Dictionary.com

Hope

(Noun)…..The feeling that what is wanted can be had or that events will turn out for the best.
(Verb)…….To look forward to with desire and reasonable confidence. To believe, desire or trust.
-Dictionary.com

Hope comes from having a purpose. "For I know the plans I have for you, declares the Lord; plans to prosper you and not to harm you, plans to give you a hope and a future." (Jeremiah 29:11)

Always be ready to give a defense to anyone who ask you for a reason for the hope that is in you. (I Peter 3:15)

Section 1

Universal Hurt

Mary A. Brown

People are hurting all over the land;
Sickness, abuse, war and hurricane.

Hopelessness and distress are in their eyes;
Wondering and praying to survive.

Tragedy occurring so unexpected;
Leaving people feeling totally neglected.

The rich, the poor, the great and small...
Pain and sorrow visit us all.

Desperation, separation, broken and crushed;
Pushing, shoving, falling and rushed.

"Oh help us God!" is the people's cry.
They look up and ask God "why."

Reaching and searching and trying to find...
Relief, comfort, and peace of mind.

When it seems you can no longer *cope*...
There is always the presence of *hope!*

Section 2

Do you know your God-given Purpose?

"Why was I born?"

"The purpose of a man's heart are deep waters but
a man of understanding draws them out."
Proverbs 20:5 (KJV)

"Before I formed you in the womb I knew you,
before you were born I set you apart..."
Jeremiah 1:5 (NIV)

"Many are the plans in a man's heart, but it is
the Lord's purpose that prevails."
Proverbs 19:21 (KJV)

Purpose

Think about It!

Purpose answers the question *"Why was I born?"*
It would be a tragedy for you to live and die without
discovering why you were sent to the earth.
God is the only one who knows your purpose for being sent
to the earth. He created you and only He knows "why".
You are not a mistake. You are here because of purpose.
God has placed greatness inside of you and the
world is waiting for you to release it!
Purpose is the source of fulfillment and knowing
your purpose will give you hope.
You can discover your purpose and meaning for your life
only when you develop a relationship with God.

God has given us a certain amount of time to fulfill our purpose.
Therefore, don't procrastinate! Don't waste your time!
Discover your purpose and get started releasing your potential today!

Section 3

Your Relationship with God

Relationship is the way in which two or more concepts, objects, or people are connected, or the state of being connected.
-Dictionary.com

Do you not know that God desires to have a *relationship* with you?

Without a *relationship* with God you have no hope for fulfilling your purpose in life.

Remember

God created you to live in *relationship* with Him.

Know what you believe about God and The Christian Doctrine

This is the Christian Doctrine that most Christians believe:

The Historic Christian Doctrine

The Holy Bible
The Holy Bible is the inspired Word of God and is the final authority for doctrine and truth.
2 Timothy 3:16; 2 Peter 1:20-21; Proverbs 30:5; Romans 16:25-26

The Trinity
We believe that there are three persons in one God; the Father, the Son and the Holy Ghost (Holy Spirit).
Matthew 28:19

The Father
We believe in God, the Father Almighty, the Author and Creator of all things.
Genesis 1:1; John 1:1

The Son

We believe that Jesus Christ is the Son of God. The Second person in the Godhead of the Trinity or Tribune Godhead.
John 1:1-14

The Holy Spirit

We believe the Holy Ghost or Holy Spirit is the third person of the Trinity, proceeds from the Father and the Son, is of the same substance, equal in power and glory, and is, together with the Father and the Son, to be believed in and obeyed. The Holy Ghost is a gift bestowed upon believers for the purpose of equipping and empowering the believers, making them more effective witnesses for service in the world. John 16:13; Acts 1:8

Salvation

We believe that we are saved by grace, through faith in Christ's death, burial, and resurrection.
Romans 10:9-10; Ephesians 2:8-9; Titus 3:5

Christ's Blood

We believe that the blood of the sinless Christ is 100 per cent sufficient to forgive men of all sins.
1 John 1:7; Revelation 1:5-9

Virgin Birth

We believe that Jesus was conceived by God by the Holy Spirit in the Virgin Mary's womb.
Matthew 1:18-20; Luke 1:31-35

Heaven and Hell

We believe that there are only two destinations for man. Eternity in heaven with God or in hell in the conscious torment....Hebrew 9:27; Matthew 25:35,41; Psalms 9:17; Psalms 103:19; Isaiah 5:14; Revelation 20:13-15

Resurrection

We believe that Jesus was physically resurrected in a glorified body, as all true believers will be one day.
Luke 24:36-39; John 2:19-21; 1 Corinthians15:42-44

Second Coming of Christ

We believe that at a time undisclosed by the Bible, Jesus will physically and visibly return to the earth.

Revelation 1:7; Acts 1:9-11; Matthew 24:30; I Thessalonians 4:15-18

Note: *All scriptures are taken from the King James Version of the Bible*

The Person and Work of the Holy Spirit (Holy Ghost)

Who is the Holy Spirit?

The Holy Spirit is a person. He is the third person of the tribune God. (Father, Son and Holy Spirit).
The "Holy Ghost" is an English variation for "Holy Spirit".

The Holy Spirit acts as a person:

- He dwells in believers. (John 14:17)
- He convicts of sin. (John 16:8)
- He inspires scripture and speaks through it. (Acts 1:16)
- He teaches and He brings to remembrance. (John 14:26)
- He guides into all truth; He speaks; He hears. (John 16:13)
- He calls to the ministry. (Acts 13:2)
- He forbids certain actions. (Acts 16:6-7)

The Holy Spirit can be treated like a person:

- He can be lied to. (Acts 5:3)
- He can be tempted. (Acts 5:9)
- He can be grieved. (Ephesian 4:30)
- He can be resisted. (Acts 7:51)
- He can be blasphemed against. (Matthew 12:31)

The Holy Spirit brings us four things:

- He brings us comfort. (John 14:16)
- He brings us counsel. (John 16:12-14)
- He brings us conviction. (John 16:8)
- He brings us connection. (Romans 8:26-27)

The Bible teaches that the baptism of the Holy Spirit is a gift that is available to every believer. (Acts 2)

The Holy Spirit is powerful:

- He is omnipotent-Almighty, have unlimited authority, influence and power.
- He is omnipresent-Present in all places at all times.
- He is omniscient-Having infinite awareness, understanding and insight; possessing universal or complete knowledge.

Section 4

Salvation

- Preservation or deliverance from harm, ruin or loss.
- Deliverance from sin and its consequences, believed by Christians to be brought about by faith in Christ.

-Dictionary.com

Reaching the Lost at any Cost

Jesus' earthly ministry of reaching the lost consisted of three things: Matthew 4:23-25

- Preaching
- Teaching
- Healing

The Great Commission

"Go ye therefore and teach all nations, baptizing them in the name of the Father and of the Son and of the Holy Ghost; Teaching them to observe all things whatsoever I have commanded you; and, lo, I am with you always, even unto the end of the world"

Matthew 28:19-20

The Fall of Man

Genesis 3:1-24

Adam and Eve were _targets of deception_ by the serpent in the Garden of Eden. The methods he used to _deceive_ Adam and Eve have not changed. He still strikes in these three areas:

1. Lust of the eye
2. Lust of the flesh
3. Pride of life

Satan's first approach was to _create doubt_. He asked a question: "Yea, hath God said?" or "Did God really say that?"

After creating doubt, his next move was _direct denial_: "Ye shall not surely die."

These are Satan's _basic strategies_ he uses to cause men and women; and boys and girls to stumble and fall today.

Be vigilant! Watch and pray!

Steps To Salvation

Humanity's Need

"For all have sinned and come short of the Glory of God."
Romans 3:23

Sin's Penalty

"For the wages of sin is death, but the gift of God
is eternal life in Christ Jesus our Lord."
Romans 6:23

God's Provision

"But God commend His love toward us, in that while
we were yet sinners, Christ died for us."
Romans 5:8

Humanity's Response

"That if thou shall confess with thou mouth the Lord Jesus, and shall believe in thine heart that God hath raised him from the dead, thou shall be saved."

Romans 10:9

Prayer for Salvation

<u>Romans 10:9</u>

- God loves you.
- Sin separates people from God.
- Jesus died for your sins.
- You can receive Jesus now and know God's love.

Pray this Prayer

Heavenly Father, in Jesus' name; I repent of my sins and I ask for your forgiveness. I invite Jesus into my heart to become my Lord and Savior. I believe Jesus died for my sins and was raised from the dead.

I now ask you to create within me a clean heart and renew a right spirit in me. Fill me with your Holy Spirit.

Thank you, Father, for saving me, in Jesus' name.

Amen!

Six Things God Hates

Proverbs 6:16-19

These <u>six things</u> doth the Lord hate: yea, <u>seven</u> are an abomination unto him:

- a proud look
- a lying tongue
- hands that shed innocent blood
- a heart that deviseth wicked imagination
- feet that be swift in running to mischief
- a false witness that speaketh lies
- he that soweth discord among brethren

Section 5

Lord Teach Us to Pray

<u>Jesus' Teaching on Prayer</u>

Read: Luke 11:2-4 (NIV) and Matthew 6:9-13 (KJV)

One day Jesus was praying in a certain place. When he finished, one of his disciples said to him, "Lord teach us to pray, just as John taught his disciples."

He said to them, "When you pray say:
Father, hallowed be your name,
Your kingdom come.
Give us each day our daily bread.
Forgive us our sins, for we also forgive
Everyone who sins against us.
And lead us not into temptation."
(Luke 11:2-4) NIV

Prayer Time!

Prayer is communicating with God.

You must learn how to pray. You can be taught how to pray.

Try to develop a daily, consistent, delightful time of prayer.

"And he spake a parable unto them to this end, that
men ought always to pray and not to faint."

Luke 18:1

All things are possible when you…

ASK! SEEK! KNOCK!

Read: Matthew 7:7-8 (NIV)

Ask, and it shall be given you;
Seek, and ye shall find;
Knock, and it shall be opened unto you.
For everyone that *asketh* receiveth;
And he that *seeketh,* findeth; and to him that *knocketh* it shall be opened.

If

If my people, which are called by my name, shall humble themselves, and pray, and seek my face, and turn from their wicked ways; then will I hear from heaven, and will forgive their sin, and will heal their land.

2 Chronicles 7:14

Put on the Armor of God

Ephesians 6:10-18 (NIV)

Finally, be strong in the Lord and in his mighty power. Put on the full armor of God, so that you can take your stand against the devil's schemes. For our struggle is not against flesh and blood, but against the rulers, against the authorities, against the power of this dark world and against the spiritual forces of evil in the heavenly realms. Therefore, put on the full armor of God, so that when the day of evil comes, you may be able to stand your ground, and after you have done everything to stand. Stand firm then, with *the belt of truth* buckled around your waist, with the *breastplate of righteousness* in place, and with your feet fitted with the readiness that comes from the *gospel of peace.* In addition to all this, take up the *shield of faith,* with which you can extinguish all the flaming arrows of the evil one. Take the *helmet of salvation* and the *sword of the Spirit* which is the Word of God. And pray in the Spirit on all occasions with all kinds of prayers and requests. With this in mind, be alert and always keep on praying for all the Lord's people.

The Lord's Prayer

Matthew 6:9-13

Key Thought: The Lord's Prayer is our "Model Prayer". It is the outline established by Jesus for communicating with God. The Lord's Prayer teaches us how to pray.

Each phrase of the prayer reflects a basic need in our lives and put us into the best possible position of having these needs met fully.

Phrase, Line 1

- Our Father which art in heaven.
  As you pray, call God "Father". Talk to Him simply from your heart. Listen to Him talk to you. He loves you.

Phrase, Line 2

- Hallowed be thy name.
  Hallowed means "holy", "set apart", "to praise"

  Begin your prayer with praise for who He is. Come before God with thanksgiving in your heart and praises in your mouth.

Phrase, Line 3

- Thy Kingdom come, Thy will be done in earth as it is in heaven.
  The Kingdom of God is a Kingdom in hearts of people. The Holy

Spirit fills hearts with righteousness, peace and joy. The Kingdom of God is not in word but in power.

Phrase, Line 4

- <u>Give us this day our daily bread.</u>
  Tell God exactly what you need today and expect Him to provide what you have asked for. Choose to serve God and put Him first in your life. He will see to it that all your needs are met.

Phrase, Line 5

- <u>And forgive us our debts as we forgive our debtors.</u>
  If we want God to forgive us, we must learn to forgive those who have hurt us.

Phrase, Line 6

- <u>And lead us not into temptation but deliver us from evil.</u>
  Put on the whole armor of God as described in Ephesians 6:10-17. The pieces of armor represent JESUS – The Word of God. Now you are ready to resist the devil and cause him to flee from you.

Phrase, Line 7

- <u>For thine is the Kingdom, and the power and the glory, forever.</u>
  This line leads you into praising God as you end your prayer time.

  Begin with praise and end with praise.

5 Steps When Praying to God for Help

This is the confidence I have in you God, that if I ask anything according to your will, you hear me. Because I know that you hear me, whatever I ask, I know that I will have the petition that I desire of you. (I John 5:14-15)

Step 1   Get God's attention. Cry out to him!

Step 2   Tell God your problem.

Step 3   Tell God what you want Him to do for you.

Step 4   Let Him know that you believe he is going to do it!

Step 5   Now, start thanking Him! Give Him praise!

"Heal me and I shall be healed. Save me and I shall be saved. For thou art my praise." (Jeremiah 17:14)

The Compound Names of God

Understanding the name of God will help you understand how to worship him more effectively.

Father God's personal name is Yahweh (Yah-way). When the Jewish people refer to the God of the Bible, they call Him "Ha Shem" (The Name) or "Adonai" (Lord, Master).

Jewish scholars began to write "Yahweh" as "Jehovah" during the time between 6th and 10th centuries.

"Yahweh" or "Jehovah" means "I will be what I will be" or "I Am who I Am"

- Jehovah Jireh (Je-ho'-vah Yeer'-eh)   The Lord Our Provider
- Jehovah Rophe (Je-ho'-vah Ro'-feh)   The Lord Our Healer
- Jehovah Nissi (Je-ho'-vah Nis'see)   The Lord My Banner
- Jehovah Tsevaot (Je-ho'-vah Tseh-vah-ot')   The Lord of Host or Lord of the armies
- Jehovah M'Kaddesh (Je-ho'-vah M'kad'-desh)   The Lord who Sanctifies You
- Jehovah Shalom (Je-ho'-vah Shal-lom)   The Lord Our Peace
- Jehovah Tsidkenu (Je-ho'-vah Sid-keh'-noo)   The Lord Our Righteousness
- Jehovah Shammah (Je-ho'-vah Shah-mah)   The Lord Who is Present
- Jehovah Rohi (Je-ho'-vah Ro'ee)   The Lord My Shepherd

Seven Basic Principles of Prayer

Principle is a fundamental truth or proposition that serves as the foundation for a system of belief or behavior or for a chain of reasoning. -Dictionary.com

1. Pray what the Bible says. (Matthew 6:10)
2. Stay in an attitude of prayer. (I Thessalonians 5:17)
3. Pray with faith. (James 1:6-8)
4. Pray bold prayers. (Hebrews 4:16)
5. Pray with fervor. (James 5:16)
6. Pray with focus. Be specific. (Matthew 6:9-13)
7. Pray for all of your needs. (Matthew 7:7)

Prayer Watches

The Bible speaks of "watches" which are specific times of the day or night.

The history of the Prayer Watches started in Jewish Calendar. The night was divided into military hours with the intent that soldiers would be on guard during these different time periods. The watches were initially divided into three watches. The Roman government increased the number of watches to four. There are four watches of the night and four watches of the day.

"Take ye heed watch and pray: for ye know not when the time is."

<u>Mark 13:33</u>

<u>Night</u>

First Watch	6 P.M. to 9 P.M.	– The Evening Watch
Second Watch	9 P.M. to 12 A.M.	– Night Seeking Watch
Third Watch	12 A.M. to 3 A.M.	– Breakthrough Watch
Fourth Watch	3 A.M. to 6 A.M.	– Morning Watch

<u>Day</u>

Fifth Watch.	6 A.M. to 9 A.M.	– Breakthrough Watch
Sixth Watch	9 A.M. to 12 P.M.	– Morning Watch
Seventh Watch . . .	12 P.M. to 3 P.M.	– Supernatural Watch
Eighth Watch	3 P.M. to 6 P.M.	– Afternoon Watch

Pray for our World

As Christians we are instructed by God to pray for those in authority.

"Therefore, I exhort first of all that supplications, prayers, intercessions, and giving of thanks be made for all men, for kings and all who are in authority, that we may lead a quiet and peaceable life in all godliness and reverence. For this is good and acceptable in the sight of God our Savior, who desires all men to be saved and to come to the knowledge of the truth. *I Timothy 2:1-4*

Pray for:

- President and his staff
- Senate, Congress, Supreme Court
- State and local governmental officials
- The Military
- Churches, Pastors, Missionaries
- School Administrators, teachers, and children
- Community leaders
- Families
- Business owners
- Others

The Jabez Prayer

I Chronicles 4:10

The name Jabez is a Hebrew baby name. In Hebrew the meaning
of the name Jabez is Pain. In the Old Testament Jabez was
so named because he was borne by his mother in Pain.
In 1 Chronicles, Jabez is a well-respected man whose
prayer to God for blessings was answered.

And Jabez called on the God of Israel saying...

"Oh, that You would bless me indeed,
And enlarge my territory,
That Your hand would be with me,
And that You would keep me from evil.
That I may not cause pain!

So God granted him what he requested.

Positions in Praying

Standing Position Mark 11:25

"Whenever you stand praying, forgive if you have anything against anyone, so that your Father who is in heaven will also forgive you your trespasses.

Sitting Position I Chronicles 17:16

"Then David the King went in and sat before the Lord and said, "Who am I, O Lord God, and what is my house that You have brought me this far?"

Kneeling Position Luke 22:41

"And He withdrew from them about a stone's throw, and He knelt down and began to pray."

Bowing Position Nehemiah 8:6

"Then Ezra blessed the Lord the great God. And all the people answered, "Amen, Amen!" while lifting up their hands; then they bowed low and worshiped the Lord with their faces to the ground."

Exodus 34:8

Moses made haste to bow low toward the earth and worship

Prostrate Matthew 26:39

"And He went a little beyond them and fell on His face and prayed, saying, "My Father, if it is possible, let this cup pass from Me; yet not as I will, but as You will."

With Uplifted Hands Position…Psalms 63:4

"So I will bless You as long as I live; I will lift up my hands in Your name."

I Timothy 2:8

"Therefore, I want the men in every place to pray, lifting up holy hands, without wrath and dissension."

Walking Position 2 Kings 4:35

"Then he returned and walked in the house once back and forth, and went up and stretched himself on him; and the lad sneezed seven times and the lad opened his eyes.

Reasons You May Not Have Your Prayers Answered

Not praying according to God's will	1 John 5:14
Disobedience	Deuteronomy 1:42-45
Praying with the wrong motive	James 4:3
Secret sin	Psalms 66:18
Lust or besetting sin	Psalm 90:8
Indifference	Proverbs 1:24-28
Secret grudge in the heart against another	1 Peter 2:1,2
Neglect of Mercy	Proverbs 21:13
Show no diligence to assist God in the answer	2 Thessalonians 3:10
Despising God's Law	Proverbs 28:8
Accusing God of deafness	Isaiah 58:3
Blood-guiltiness	Isaiah 1:1
Iniquity in your heart	Isaiah 59:2; Psalm 66:18
Stubbornness	Zechariah 7:13
Instability/Lack of Faith	James 11:6-7
Self-Indulgence	James 4:3

Fasting and Praying

The Old and New Testaments teach the value of *fasting*
and *praying* in order to seek God's will for our lives.
It has been discovered that God gives supernatural
revelation and wisdom through *fasting* and *praying*.
We can develop a closer relationship with God through *fasting*.

Joel 2:12 says: "Even now, declares the Lord, return to me with
all your heart, with *fasting* and *weeping* and *mourning*."

Hippocrates

Father of Modern Medicine

Hippocrates taught people to rely upon diet
and exercise more than upon drugs.

He also taught that man should eat only one meal a day.

He often prescribed

Fasting.

God's Call to Fast and Pray

Isaiah 58:6 (KJV)

<u>Is this not the fast I have chosen?</u>

- To loose the bands of wickedness.
- To undo the heavy burdens.
- To let the oppressed go free.
- To break every yoke.

<u>What is Biblical Fasting?</u>

- Biblical fasting is going without food. It means the voluntary abstinence from food.
- Fasting is a matter of the heart, not a matter of outward appearance.
- Fasting puts us in a position to know what is missing, broken, damaged or out of balance in our lives.
- Prayer puts us into a greater reliance upon the Lord to heal, restore, reconcile, balance or create what we need for balance and wholeness.

<u>The Bible describes four major types of fasting, and they are:</u>

<u>A Regular Fast</u>.....Traditionally, a regular fast means refraining from eating all food. Most people drink water or juice during a regular fast.

<u>A Partial Fast</u>........This type of fast generally refers to omitting a specific meal from your diet or refraining from certain types of foods. <u>See:</u> Daniel

1:12 (vegetables & water). Daniel 10:2-3 (No choice food, no meat or wine).

A Full Fast..............These fasts are complete...no food and no drink.

See: Esther 4:15-16 (no food & no drink for 3 days).

Sexual/Marriage Fast.....I Corinthians 7:3-6 says… "Do not deprive each other except by mutual consent and for a time, so that you may devote yourselves to prayer. Then come together again so that Satan will not tempt you because of your lack of self-control."

Suggested Scriptures to read during your fast

- James 1:6-8
- Psalms 18:2
- Hebrews 4:16
- Psalms 70:5
- Galatians 5:19-21
- Psalms 2:8
- John 14:14
- 2 Samuel 22:2-4
- Psalms 40:17
- James 5:14-16
- 2 Chronicles 7:14

Note: *Stay in the Word when you fast and pray.*

Oil

The oil used in conjunction with prayer becomes miracle healing oil.

<u>Why Oil?</u>

Oil symbolizes the Spirit

- Aaron, the High Priest was anointed with oil. Psalms 133:3
- David, the King was anointed with oil. Psalms 23:5
- The tabernacles, the congregation, the ark, the table and all holy vessels were anointed with oil. Exodus 30:25-29
- The Apostles of Christ used oil to heal the sick and they cast out many devils, and anointed with oil many that were sick and healed them. Mark 6:13
- James 5:13-14 says: "Is any among you afflicted? Let him pray. Is any merry? Let him sing psalms. Is any sick among you? Let him call for the elders of the church; and let them pray over him, anointing him with oil in the name of the Lord."

A prayer for blessing the oil

Our Father in heaven, you brought healing to the sick through your son Jesus Christ.

We believe in your power to heal and we ask that you would send the Holy Spirit to bless this oil. May everyone anointed with this oil receive the blessing they desire of you. Cause them to be healed of their pain, trauma, sickness, diseases, infirmities and hurts. Let divine order be established in the life of everyone who will be anointed with this oil.

In Jesus' name we pray. Thank you Jesus! Amen!

*(Keep a Daily Record of your prayer requests and record
the faithfulness of God in answering your prayers)*

A Prayer Chart

My Name:_____

Date: _____
My Prayer Request

How did God answer?

Date: _____
My Prayer Request

How did God answer?

Date: _____
My Prayer Request

How did God answer?

My Commitment to Daily Prayer

Beginning date: _____

I, _____ agree to pray

Your name

for at least one hour daily.

(You may divide the one hour into 15 minutes or 30 minutes intervals)

A commitment to daily prayer helps to develop
Holy Discipline and Great Power.

Section 6

Save Our Children Outreach (SOCO)

"A Child Saved is A Life Saved"

- Children are important to God.
- They are a valuable part of God's Kingdom.

"A woman giving birth to a child has *pain* because her time has come; but when her baby is born she forgets the anguish because of her joy that a child is born into the world."
John 16:21

The Family Prayer Challenge

The Challenge

Start praying The Lord's Prayer in your home with your children daily!

Purpose

For the saving and protection of our children

The Lord's Prayer

Matthew 6:9-13(KJV)

Our Father which art in heaven
Hallowed be thy name.

Thy Kingdom come, Thy will be done
In earth, as it is in heaven.

Give us this day our daily bread.
Forgive us our debts, as we forgive our debtors.

And lead us not into temptation
But deliver us from evil.

For thine is the Kingdom,
And the power and the glory, forever.

_Amen _

Blessing The Children

Mark 10:13-16 (NIV)

People were bringing little children to Jesus for him to place his hands on them, but the disciples rebuked them. When Jesus saw this He was indignant. He said to them, "Let the little children come to me, and do not hinder them, for the Kingdom of God belongs to such as these."

Truly I tell you, anyone who will not receive the Kingdom of God like a little child will never enter it: And He took the children in His arms, placed His hands on them and blessed them.

"See that you do not despise one of these little ones; for I tell you that their angels in heaven always see the face of my Father in heaven."

Matthew 18:10 (NIV)

Behold, children are a heritage from the Lord, and the fruit of the womb is his reward; as arrows are in the hands of a mighty man; so are children of the youth. Happy is the man that hath his quiver full of them; they shall not be ashamed but they shall speak with the enemies in the gate.
Psalms 127:3-5 (KJV)

(When we pray God's Word, we are actually
praying the will and mind of God).

Pray God's Word Over the Children

- I pray that our children will know and remember that Jesus has come to seek and to save that which was lost. (Luke 19:10)
- I pray that if our children will confess with their mouth the Lord Jesus and believe in their heart that God raised Him from the dead, they will be saved. (Romans 10:9-10)
- I pray that our children will not be conformed to this world, but that they will be transformed by the renewing of their minds. (Romans 12:2)
- I pray that our children will present their bodies as a living sacrifice, holy and acceptable to You, God.
  (Romans 12:1)
- I pray that You God will be merciful to our children according to your word. (Psalms 119:58)
- I pray that our children shall know the truth and the truth shall make them free. (John 8:32)
- I pray that no weapon formed against our children shall prosper and every tongue which rises against them in judgement, You God shall condemn.(Isaiah 54:17)
- I pray that our children will be doers of your word and not hearers only. (James 1:22)
- I pray that You, Jesus are always at our children's right hand, that they may not be shaken. (Acts 2:25)
- I pray that our children who walk in the law of the Lord, will be blessed. (Psalms 119:1)
- I pray that if our children confess their sin, You, God are faithful and just to forgive their sin and to cleanse them from all unrighteousness. (I John 1:9)

- I pray that You, God will blot out our children's transgressions for your own sake and that you will not remember their sin. (Isaiah 43:25)
- I pray that You, God will give your angels charge over our children to keep them in all their ways. (Psalms 91:11)
- I pray that You, Lord are our children's helper and they will not fear. (Hebrews 13:6)
- I pray that our children know that You have not given them a spirit of fear, but of power and of love and of a sound mind. (II Timothy 1:7)
- I pray that no evil shall befall our children. (Psalms 9:10)

Make These Declarations Over Your Children Daily!

I decree and declare......

Our children are gifts from God. They are not a mistake.
Our children have the mind of Christ.
God's goodness will continue on our children.
God's hands protect our children daily.
The Lord will give our children peace.
The joy of the Lord is our children's strength.
Our children are our greatest blessing.
The future is blessed for our children.
Our children will choose life and not death.
Our children will make wise choices in life.
Jesus paid the price for our children's salvation.
Our children are destined for greatness.
Our children are the head and not the tail.
Our children will live in prosperity all their lives.
Our children will walk in health.
Our children's needs are met daily.

Section 7

Let's go back to the Bible!

THE WORD of GOD

"In the beginning was the Word, and the Word was with God, and the Word was God."

John 1:18

"For the Word of God is quick, and powerful and sharper than any two edge sword; piercing even to the dividing asunder of soul and spirit and the joints and marrow and is a discerner of the thoughts and intent of the heart."

Hebrews 4:12

It's Time to be Enthusiastic about God's Word

Enthusiasm comes from two Greek words:
"en" (in) and "theos" (God)

Enthusiasm is the inspiration that makes you wake up and live.

Enthusiasm will cause you to sing and others will sing with you.

If you do not have *"enthusiasm"* you need to pray and ask God for it.

Enthusiastic

1. Intense and eager enjoyment, interest or approval.
2. Religious fervor supposedly resulting directly from divine inspiration.

It is time to study your Bible

A Time for Everything

Ecclesiastes 3:1-12 KJV
"There is a time for everything and a season
for every purpose under heaven."

A time to be born and a time to die.

A time to plant and a time to pluck up.

A time to kill and time to heal.

A time to break down and a time to build up.

A time to weep and time to laugh.

A time to mourn and a time to dance.

A time to cast away stones and a time to gather stones.

A time to embrace and a time to refrain from embracing.

A time to get and a time to lose.

A time to keep and a time to throw away.
A time to rend and a time to sew.

A time to be silent and a time to speak.

A time to love and a time to hate.

A time of war and a time of peace.

He hath made everything beautiful in His time.
And.......
(It is time to start studying the Word of God!!!)

Do you know your Bible?

IQ

1. What is the Bible?
    (The word "Bible" comes from the Greek word "biblia" meaning "books." It is a collection of ancient writings about God – Yahweh)

2. What are the two main parts of the Bible?
    (The two main parts of the Bible are: Old Testament and New Testament)

3. What does the word "testament" mean?
    (Testament means "agreement")

4. What does "scripture" mean?
    (Scripture means "sacred writings")

5. Who wrote the Bible?
    (The Bible was written by many different inspired authors, mostly Hebrews, some unknown)

6. When was the Bible written?
    (The Bible was written at different times and at different places)

7. How many books are there in the Bible?
    (There are 39 books in the Old Testament...Contains stories about an Old Agreement between God and the Hebrews, as revealed to their leader Moses)

(There are 27 books in the New Testament…Contains stories and teachings about a New Agreement between God and people based on the teachings of the life of Jesus)

A total of 66 books in the Bible.

The Bible

(Greek "biblia" books)

- The greatest book ever written is the Bible. It is a book of divine instructions.
- The Bible deals with spiritual matters. Therefore, it requires personal illumination by the Holy Spirit to understand it.
- The Bible is not just one book – It is an entire library of books. It is also a collection of ancient writings about God (Yahweh).
- The Bible has one true author and that author is God.
- All or part of the Bible has been translated into more than 1,200 languages.
- There are 1,189 chapters in the Old & New Testaments
- The main theme of the Bible is the Lord Jesus Christ and His work of redemption for mankind.
- God has given the Bible in order that we might know Him and that we might do His work on earth.

All scriptures are given by inspiration of God and is profitable for doctrine, for reproof, for correction, and for instruction in righteousness.

(2 Timothy 3:16)

Be doers of the Word and not hearers only. (James 1:22)

Old Testament Literature

Pentateuch "pen te' took" – The Torah

The first five books in the Old Testament are The Books of Moses

<u>Moses</u>

- Genesis – 50 chapters
- Exodus – 40 chapters
- Leviticus – 27 chapters
- Numbers – 36 chapters
- Deuteronomy – 34 chapters

<u>History</u>

- Joshua – 24 chapters
- Judges – 21 chapters
- Ruth – 4 chapters
- I Samuel – 31 chapters
- 2 Samuel – 24 chapters
- I Kings – 22 chapters
- 2 Kings – 25 chapters
- 1 Chronicles – 29 chapters
- 2 Chronicles – 36 chapters
- Ezra – 10 chapters
- Nehemiah – 13 chapters
- Esther – 10 chapters

<u>Poetry</u>

- Job – 42 chapters
- Psalms – 150 chapters
- Proverbs – 31 chapters
- Ecclesiastes – 12 chapters
- Song of Solomon – 8 chapters

<u>Major Prophets</u>

- Isaiah – 66 chapters
- Jeremiah – 52 chapters
- Lamentations – 5 chapters
- Ezekiel – 48 chapters
- Daniel – 12 chapters

<u>Minor Prophets</u> (Called minor because of the length of their writings)

- Hosea – 14 chapters
- Joel – 3 chapters
- Amos – 9 chapters
- Obadiah – 1 chapter
- Jonah – 4 chapters
- Micah -7 chapters
- Nahum – 3 chapters
- Habakkuk – 3 chapters
- Zephaniah -3 chapters
- Haggai – 2 chapters
- Zechariah – 14 chapters
- Malachi – 4 chapters

New Testament Literature

Historical

- Matthew – 28 chapters
- Mark -16 chapters
- Luke – 24 chapters
- John – 21 chapters
- Acts – 28 chapters

Epistolary

- Romans – 16 chapters
- 1 Corinthians – 16 chapters
- 2 Corinthians – 13 chapters
- Galatians – 6 chapters
- Ephesians – 6 chapters
- Philippians – 4 chapters
- Colossians – 4 chapters
- I Thessalonians – 5 chapters
- 2 Thessalonians – 3 chapters
- I Timothy – 6 chapters
- 2 Timothy – 3 chapters
- Titus – 3 chapters
- Philemon – 1 chapter
- Hebrews – 13 chapters
- James – 5 chapters
- 1 Peter – 5 chapters
- 2 Peter – 3 chapters

- 1 John – 5 chapters
- 2 John – 1 chapter
- 3 John – 1 chapter
- Jude – 1 chapter

<u>Prophetical</u>

- Revelation – 22 chapters

Why read the Bible?

- Read to help you understand God and God's work.
- Read to help you know how to live and act.
- Read to share stories of human experiences in many literary forms.
- Read to know about the most famous book in history.

How to read the Bible

- Set aside time for Bible reading daily.
- Read a certain number of chapters daily.
- Keep a notebook or journal.
- Keep a dictionary and other study tools with you as you read.
- Try to understand the writer's purpose.
- Try to understand who the message is for.
- Always pray before you began reading the Bible. Ask the Holy Spirit to guide you as you study.

Some of the Best Known Bible Versions and Translations

- <u>American Standard Version (ASV)</u>
  Also known as the Standard American Edition Revised Version, is a revised version of the KJV.

- <u>New International Version (NIV)</u>
  Combination word-for-word and thought-for-thought translation.

- <u>King James Version (KJV)</u>
  The first version of Scripture authorized by the Protestant Church and commissioned by England's King James I word-for-word.

- <u>New King James Version(NKJ)</u>
  A modern language update of the original King James Version.

- <u>New Living Translation (NLT)</u>
  A Modern English translation focusing on producing clarity in the meaning of the text.

- <u>New Revised Standard (NRS)</u>
  A popular translation that follows in the traditions of the King James and Revised Standard Versions.

- <u>Revised Standard Version (RSV)</u>
  A revision of the King James Version, the Revised Version, and American Standard Version.

- English Standard Version (ESV)
  A relatively new Bible translation that combine word-for-word precision and accuracy with literary excellence, beauty, and readability word-for-word.

- Good News Translation (GNT)
  First published in 1976 by the American Bible Society in a "common language."

- Holman Christian Standard (CSB)
  A highly readable, accurate translation written in modern English.

- The Message (MSG)
  A paraphrase from the original languages written by Eugene H. Peterson.

- New American Standard (NAS)
  Written in a formal style but is more readable than the King James Version.

- Douay-Rheims (RHE)
  The translation upon which nearly all English Catholic Bible Versions are based.

- Lexicons
  Provides definitions and meaning of Biblical words found in the original New Testament Greek and Old Testament Hebrew language of the Holy Bible. Additional, lexicons give the context and cultural meaning intended by the authors.

Suggested Bible Study Tools

- *Organize your own personal library and study area with some of the study tools listed below*
- <u>Bible</u>.........Select a version or translation you are comfortable with.
- <u>Interlinear Bible</u> makes it quicker to determine the Hebrew or Greek meaning.
- <u>Bible Dictionary and a Standard Dictionary</u>
- <u>Concordance</u>s......The alphabetical index of words in a book or in an author's works with the passages in which they occur.
- <u>Commentaries</u>.....Written by well known theologians, providing explanation and interpretation of Bible scriptures.
- <u>Map</u>s help to locate the places referenced, understand distances and perceive relationships between them.
- Suggested: Nelson's Complete Book of Bible Maps and Charts

Pray the Scripture Against FEAR

Fear is an unpleasant emotion caused by the belief that someone or something is dangerous, likely to cause pain or a threat.
-Dictionary.com-

- For God has not given us a spirit of fear, but of power and of love and of a sound mind.
  2 Timothy 1:7

- There is no fear in love. But perfect love drives out fear, because fear has to do with punishment. The one who fear is not made perfect in love.
  I John 4:18

- But now, this is what the Lord say…Fear not, for I have redeemed you; I have summoned you by name; you are mine.
  Isaiah 43:1

- Even though I walk through the valley of the shadow of death, I will fear no evil for you are with me; your rod and your staff they comfort me.
  Psalms 23:4

- So do not fear for I am with you; do not be dismayed for I am your God. I will strengthen you and help you: I will uphold you with my righteous right hand.
  Isaiah 41:10

- When I am afraid, I put my trust in you.
  Psalms 56:3

- Peace is what I leave with you; it is my own peace that I give you.
  I do not give it as the world does. Do not be worried and upset;
  do not be afraid.
  John 14:27

- The Lord is with me; I will not be afraid. What can man do to
  me? The Lord is with me; He is my helper.
  Psalms 118:6-7

- The angel of the Lord encamps around those who fear him and
  delivers them.
  Psalms 34:7

- I prayed to the Lord and He answered me. He freed me from all
  my fears.
  Psalms 34:4

- Do not be afraid of them; the Lord your God himself will fight
  for you.
  Deuteronomy 3:22

- Jesus told him, don't be afraid; just believe.
  Mark 5:36

- The Lord is my light and my salvation, who shall I fear? The Lord
  is the strength of my life, of whom shall I be afraid?
  Psalms 27:1

- Be strong and courageous. Do not be afraid or terrified because of
  them, for the Lord your God goes with you; He will never leave
  you nor forsake you.
  Deuteronomy 31:6

- Tell everyone who is discouraged, Be strong and don't be afraid. God is coming to your rescue.
  Isaiah 35:4

F = False

E= Evidence

A= Appearing

R= Real

Healing Scriptures to Pray

- Heal me and I shall be healed. Save me and I shall be saved. For thou art my praise.
  Jeremiah 17:14

- Lord, say the word and I will be healed.
  Matthew 8:8

- Strengthen me according to Thy Word. Remove the false way from me and graciously grant me thy law.
  Psalms 119:28-29

- Lord, establish your word in me. I want your Word to renew my mind and create reverence for you.
  Psalms 119:38

- Sustain me according to Thy Word, that I may live; And do not let me be ashamed of my hope.
  Psalms 119:116

- Surely He took up our infirmities and carried our sorrows, yet we considered him stricken by God, smitten by him and afflicted. But he was wounded for our transgressions, bruised for our iniquities; the chastisement of our peace was upon him and with his stripes we are healed.
  Isaiah 53:4-5

- He sent forth His Word and healed them; He rescued them from the grave.
  Psalms 107:20

- A cheerful heart is good medicine, but a crushed spirit dries up the bones.
  Proverbs 17:22

- But for you who revere my name, the sun of righteousness will rise with healing in its wings.
  Malachi 4:2

- Praise the Lord, O my soul, and forget not all his benefits. Who forgives all your sins and heals all your diseases.
  Psalms 103:2-3

- He gives strength to the weary and increases the power of the weak.
  Isaiah 40:29

- I shall not die but live and declare the works of the Lord.
  Psalm 118:17

- And the prayer offered in faith will make the sick person well, the Lord will raise him up. If he has sinned, he will be forgiven.
  James 5:15

- He said, If you listen carefully to the voice of the Lord your God and do what is right in his eyes, if you pay attention to his commands and keep all his decrees, I will not bring on you any of the diseases I brought on the Egyptians, for I am the Lord, who heals you.
  Exodus 15:26

- But I will restore you to health and heal your wounds, declares the Lord, because you are called an outcast, Zion for whom no one cares.
  Jeremiah 30:17

- This day I call heaven and earth as witnesses against you that I have set before you life and death, blessings and curses. Now choose life so that you and your children may live.
  Deuteronomy 30:19

- This is the confidence we have in approaching God: that if we ask anything according to his will, he hears us. And if we know that he hears us, whatever we ask, we know that we have what we asked of him.
  I John 5:14-15

Healing in the Psalms

"The Hymnbook of Praise & Worship"

The purpose of the psalms is to provide poetry for the expression of praise, worship and confession to God.

- David wrote 73 Psalms
- Asaph wrote 12 Psalms
- Sons of Korah wrote 9 Psalms
- Solomon wrote 2 Psalms
- Heman with Korah, Ethan & Moses each wrote one Psalm
- 51 Psalms writers are anonymous

When you are worried read: Psalm 37

When you are confused read: Psalms 10, 12, 73

When you are sad read: Psalm 13

When you are depressed read: Psalms 27, 34, 42, 43, 88, 143

When you are tired/weak read: Psalms 6, 13, 18, 28, 29, 40, 86

When you are in trouble read: Psalms 3, 14, 22, 37:1-11, 42, 46, 53, 116:1-7

To be forgiven for your sin read: Psalm 51

The never ending story of God's love read: Psalm 136

My Commitment to Daily Bible Reading

I, _____agree

(Your name)

to read my Bible daily.

(Start with 15-30 minutes each day and gradually increase the time)

Beginning date: _____

Note: Go to this site to locate a Bible Reading Plan
http://www.bible-reading.com/bible-plan.html

Section 8

Praise and Worship

"I will bless the Lord at all times: his praise
shall continually be in my mouth."

Psalms 34:1 (KJV)

Praise and Worship

Know the Difference

There is a difference between "praise" and "worship".

Knowing and understanding the difference between praise and worship can bring a new depth to the way we honor the Lord.

Without "praise" there is no "presence" and without "presence" there is no "worship".

"Praise" is something we do while "worship" is something God releases.

Therefore, the mingling of God's presence with our praise is called "worship."

Praise can be a part of worship, but worship goes beyond praise.

God invites praise of all kinds from His creation. Jesus said, "If my people don't praise God, even the rocks will cry out" Luke 19:40

Worship is a lifestyle, not just an occasional activity. Jesus said the Father is seeking those who will worship Him in spirit and in truth.

Worship comes from a different place within our spirit. Worship should be reserved for God alone. (Luke 4:8)

Worship requires that we be willing to humble ourselves before God, surrender every part of our lives to His control and adore Him for who He is not just what He has done.

Worship involves "intimacy."

Praise

(Praising God will get you healed)

<u>What is Praise?</u>

- Praise is an outward expression of one's love and appreciation to God.
- Praise is a spiritual weapon.
- Praise brings God on the scene, for He inhabits the praise of His people.
- Praise is always positive. There is no such thing as negative praise.
- Praise is something we can do anytime and anywhere.
- Praise turns our attention from ourselves to God.
- Praise can always be seen or heard. It cannot be kept silent.

Seven Hebrew Words for Praise

- Halal (haw-lal)   to celebrate; to boast, to shine, to make a show, to be clamorously foolish.

- Barak (Baw-rak)   to kneel; to bless God (as an act of adoration).

- Shabach (shaw-bakh)   to address in a loud tone.

- Thillah (the-hil-law)   to sing, laudation, a hymn, praise.

- Towdah (to-daw)   an extension of the hand, sacrifice of praise.

- Yadah (yaw-daw)   hold out hands, to revere or worship with extended hands.

- Zamar (zaw-mar)   to touch the strings or parts of a musical instrument, i.e. play upon it, to make music accompanied by the voice, hence to celebrate in song and music, give praise, sing forth praises and psalms.

Dance your way through your pain and hurts

Dance

- You have turned for me my mourning into <u>dancing;</u> You have loosed my sackcloth and girded me with gladness. (Psalms 30:11)
- Let them praise His name with <u>dancing</u>; Let them sing praises to Him with timbrel and lyre. (Psalms 149:3)
- Praise Him with timbrel and <u>dancing</u>; Praise Him with stringed instruments and pipe. (Psalms 150:4)
- A time to weep and a time to laugh; A time to mourn and a time to <u>dance.</u> (Ecclesiastes 3:4)
- David was <u>dancing</u> before the Lord with all his might and he was wearing a linen ephod. (2 Samuel 6:14)

Shout your way through your pain and hurts

Shout

- Be glad in the Lord and rejoice you righteous ones; And shout for joy all you who are upright in heart. (Psalms 32:11)
- Let them shout for joy and rejoice who favor my vindication; And let them say continually, "The Lord be magnified, who delights in the prosperity of His servant." (Psalms 35:27)
- O clap your hands all ye people; Shout to God with the voice of joy. (Psalms 47:1)
- Shout joyfully to God, all the earth. (Psalms 66:1)
- Shout joyfully to the Lord all the earth; Break forth and sing for joy and sing praises. (Psalms 98:4)
- Shout joyfully to the Lord all the earth. (Psalms 100:1)

Sing your way through your pain and hurts

Sing

- Sing for joy to God our strength; Shout joyfully to the God of Jacob. Raise a song, strike the timbrel, the sweet sounding lyre with the harp. (Psalms 81:1-2)
- I will sing of the loving kindness of the Lord forever; To all generations I will make known your faithfulness with my mouth. (Psalms 89:1)
- O sing to the Lord a new song, for He has done wonderful things; His right hand and His holy arm have gained the victory for Him. (Psalms 98:1)
- Sing to the Lord a new song; Sing to the Lord all the earth. Sing to the Lord, bless His name; Proclaim good tidings of His salvation from day to day. (Psalms 96:1-2)
- I will sing a new song to you, O God; Upon a harp of ten strings I will sing praises to you. (Psalms 144:9-10)

Nine basic acts of praising God

Three ways of praising Him with the mouth:

- Testimonies
- Sing
- Shout unto Him

Three ways of praising Him with the hands:

- Lifting of hands (symbol of surrender or submission)
- Applaud or Clapping (I appreciate you)
- Playing musical instruments

Three ways of praising Him with the body (posture):

- Standing in His presence – Honor God in reverence
- Kneeling or bowing (Our bodies and hearts)
- Dancing

Reasons to praise Him

- Praise Him for his faithfulness to you .... Psalms 89:5
- Praise Him for his excellent greatness .... Psalms 150:2
- Praise Him for his mighty act .... Psalms 150:2
- Praise Him for his goodness .... Psalms 135:2
- Praise Him for saving you .... Psalms 103:2-3
- Praise Him for healing you .... Jeremiah 17:14
- Praise Him for protecting you .... Psalms 119:116
- Praise Him for the gift of the Holy Spirit .... I John 5:14-15

Note: Try to think of other reasons to praise God.

Let's Worship the Lord

"But an hour is coming and now is when the true worshipers will worship the Father in Spirit and Truth; for such people the Father seeks to be His worshipers." John 4:23

<u>What is Worship?</u>

- Worship is the way we minister unto God when we get into His presence.
- Worship is to pay homage (honor) to God.
- Worship is to lower or prostrate oneself in the presence of God in surrender and submission to Him.
- Worship is reverence, a feeling of profound respect, mingled with awe and wonder.
- Worship is to give God first place in our lives and to magnify him above all else.
- Worship is willingness to give to God all that He requires.
- Worship is inward (heart); internal.

Ways in which worshipers worship

- By prostrating..............................I Kings 18:39
- Bowing to the ground.................Genesis 18:1-2
- With uplifted hands ....Psalms 63:4
- Kneeling before Him..................Psalms 95:6
- Dancing before Him...................2 Samuel 6:14
- Clapping hands ....Psalms 47:1
- With eyes lifted up ....Psalms 123:1
- With a loud voice.......................Psalms 19:37
- With Musical instruments ....Psalms 150:1-6

Note: All scriptures are taken from the NASB

Remember!

- The Lord has created us to be worshipers. This is our first and highest calling.
- God lives in an atmosphere of praise.
- Praise is a mighty weapon against the enemy.
- If you desire to please God then strive to be a "true worshiper" of His.

My Commitment to Daily Praise and Worship

I, _____agree,

your name

to make time to praise and worship the Lord daily.

"I will sing a new song unto thee, O God"

Psalms 144:9 (KJV)

Section 9

#1 Key to Healing is Forgive and be Healed

*"Forbearing one another, and forgiving one another,
if any man have a quarrel against any; even as Christ
forgave you, so also do ye." Colossians 3:13 (KJV)*

- Let go of all bitterness, resentment, envy, strife and wickedness in any form.
- Release forgiveness to all who have wronged and hurt you.
- Forgive them…Release them…Be healed!

Forgive

- To stop feeling angry or resentful toward someone for an offense, flaw, or mistake.
- To pardon, excuse, exonerate, absolve, cancel a debt, wipe the slate clean.
- We forgive others when we let go of resentment and give up any claim to be compensated for the hurt or loss we have suffered.

Forgiveness

- Giving up my right to hurt you, for hurting me.
- To release a person from the wrong they committed against us.
- The act of pardoning an offender.
- The Greek word translated "forgiveness" literally means "to let go."
- Forgiveness is an act of our own personal will in obedience and submission to God's will, trusting God to bring emotional healing.

Why Forgive?

- We forgive so we won't become bitter and defile those around us.
- We forgive others to gain control of our lives from hurt emotions.
- We forgive in obedience to God. Matthew 6:14-15; Roman 12:18.
- You are not condoning the wrong or acting as if it never happened... you are simply letting it go!
- Letting go of anger and resentment can help you to keep calm, improve your health and increase your happiness.

- By forgiving others, we free ourselves spiritually and emotionally.
- It is important to remember that forgiveness is not granted because a person deserves to be forgiven. Instead, it is an act of love, mercy and grace.

My Forgiveness Release Page

"And forgive us our trespasses, as we forgive them that trespass against us." Matthew 6:12 (KJV)
I have chosen to release forgiveness to the following person(s) who have caused me hurt and pain.

List the first name or the person's initials on the lines below.
After you complete your "Forgiveness Page" you may shred or burn it as a sign of total release.

_____

_____

_____

_____

_____

_____

_____

_____

_____

Signs of Hurt and Pain

- Moodiness (up & down)
- Aggression – lashes out
- Frequent temper tantrums
- Violent outbursts toward others
- Extremely quiet or withdrawn
- Alcohol & drug abuse
- Inappropriate sexual activities
- Eating disorder
- Overweight or underweight
- Threats (speak out)
- Low self-esteem or low self-worth
- Anxiety attacks
- Excessive complaining
- Offensive body odor
- Untidy clothing
- Without hope; unhappy
- Self-derogatory thoughts
- Changes in body language
- Low mood (e.g. suicidal thoughts or intents)
- Depression
- Change in sleeping habits
- Extremely perfectionistic
- Attempts to fulfill everyone's expectations
- Resentful
- Bitter
- Excessive fear
- Bizarre behavior

- Craving attention & affection
- Personality change
- Wanting to manipulate & control others
- Making excuses; blaming
- Poor impulse control
- Talkative
- Watch facial expressions (frowning, sad, etc.)

Hurt people need one another

The Bible tells us how we are to treat one another

- For this is the message you heard from the beginning, that we should love one another. I John 3:11
- Don't grumble against one another, brothers and sisters or you will be judged. James 5:9
- So that there should be no division in the body, but that its parts should have equal concern for each other. I Corinthians 12:25
- If one part suffers, every part suffers with it; if one part is honored, every part rejoices with it. I Corinthians 12:26
- ...Encourage one another. I Thessalonians 4:18
- Each of you should use whatever gift you have received to serve others. I Peter 4:10
- Finally, all of you be like minded, be sympathetic, love one another, be compassionate and humble. I Peter 3:8
- And let us consider how we may spur one another on toward love and good deeds. Hebrews 10:24
- If someone is caught in a sin, you who live by the Spirit should restore that person gently. Galatians 6:1
- Follow the way of love and eagerly desire gifts of the Spirit. I Corinthians 14:1
- Teach and admonish one another with all wisdom. Colossians 3:16

Section 10

Overcomers

- <u>Overcome</u> = to conquer, to achieve a victory over defeat; to master, to beat, to prevail over, to subdue, to take, to win.
- <u>Overcomer= a person who overcomes; a person who has experienced a change in behavior or attitude after achieving a victory over defeat.</u>

Dictionary.com

My Overcomer Declaration

"I am an overcomer"

Mary A. Brown, M.Ed., D. Min.

I am an Overcomer!
God has forgiven me of all my sins.
He has placed them on the cross.
Covered them with the blood; Never to bring them up again.

I have stepped up to the plate.
I've made a decision.
I am created for greatness and
I'm not going to settle for less.

I won't give up, look back, turn around nor be afraid.
Yesterday is gone and tomorrow may never be mine.
Today is all I have.

I am tired and sick and tired of hurting!
I'm done with nursing and rehearsing my hurts.
Today, I will disperse them and let God reverse them.

I was created for more than what I have, and
I'm no longer going to settle for low living, small planning, bad dreams,
miniature visions, foolish talking, cheap living, and small goals.

I no longer need the approval of man to feel worthwhile.

My self worth is built on the love, acceptance and forgiveness of Christ.
I don't need popularity, promotion nor position. I don't need to be hugged,
kissed, praised, recognized nor rewarded.

I now know who I am and whose I am, and
I can do all things through Christ who strengthen me.

The path I've chosen is straight, narrow and rough.
My companions are few. My guide is trustworthy.

I will not be afraid of my enemies.
I will not waste my time seeking vengeance.
For vengeance is the Lord's and He will repay.

I will let go of everything and everybody who is taking from me
rather than adding to me.
I will not be defined by the opinions and lies of others.
I am too blessed to be stressed and you don't know my story.

My family, friends, associates, church folks and others,
will no longer be able to manipulate, control and rule my life.
I am an overcomer and today I will pursue, overtake and recover all!
Yes, I am an overcomer and I will not give up, I will not let up and
I will not shut up until I have taken back everything the enemy has stolen
from me.

Yes, I am an overcomer, and today I am taking back control of my life!
I am an overcomer and today is my day to celebrate!

################################

Start writing your own Overcomer Declaration

- Start by saying "I am an Overcomer."
- Focus on the hurts and anger you were dealing with in your past.

- Next, state the positive changes that have occurred in your life as a result of you having overcome your hurts and pain.
- Regardless of how small the positive change may appear; remember, "You are an overcomer!"

God's promise to the overcomers

(The Seven Churches of Asia Minor...Revelation 2:1-29; 3:1-22)

Church	Promise
Ephesus	To him that overcometh I will give to eat of the tree of life which is in the midst of the Paradise of God.
Smyrna	He that overcometh shall not be hurt of the second death.
Pergamum	To him that overcometh will I give to eat of the hidden manna and will give him a white stone and on the stone a new name written which no man know saving he that receiveth it.
Thyatira	And he that overcometh and keepeth my works unto the end to him will I give power over the nations and he shall rule them with a rod of iron and I will give him the morning star.
Sardis	He that overcometh the same shall be clothed in white raiment and I will not blot out his name out of the book of life but will confess his name before my father and before his angels.
Philadelphia	Him that overcometh will I make a pillar in the temple of my God. I will write upon him the name of my God and the name of the city of my God and I will write upon him my new name.
Laodicean	To him that overcometh will I grant to sit with me in my throne even as I also overcame and am set down with my father in His throne.

Positive Affirmations

Build Self-Esteem and Self-Worth

<u>Affirmation</u> = Positive statements that describe a desired situation or goal which are often repeated until they get impressed on the subconscious mind.

• I Am Somebody!	Jesse Jackson
• It ain't what they call you, it's what you answer to	W.C. Field
• The way you treat yourself sets the standard for others	Sonya Friedman
• Act as if what you do make a difference, It does!	William James
• Everybody is unique. Don't compare yourself with anybody else	Unknown
• Think high and you'll rise! Think low and you'll stay in a rut	Unknown
• Your time is limited, so don't waste it living someone else's life	Unknown
• Someone opinion of you does not have to become your reality	Les Brown
• Never! Never! Never give up!	Sir Winston Churchill
• Never bend your head. Hold it high. Look the world straight in the eye	Helen Keller

- No one can make you feel inferior without your consent — Eleanor Roosevelt
- You have to expect things of yourself before you can do them — Michael Jordan
- We can never do the right thing as long as we are out to please someone else — Alice Miller
- It's not your job to like me…It's mine — Byron Katie
- It is never too late to be what you might have been — George Eliot
- When you find yourself in a hole, stop digging — Will Rogers
- You have brains in your head; You have feet in your shoes. You can steer yourself any direction you choose — Dr. Seuss
- It's not what you are that holds you back, it's what you think you're not! — Denis Waitley

God grant me the
Serenity
to accept the things
I cannot change

Courage to
change the things I can

and

Wisdom to
know the difference

(The Serenity Prayer is the common name for a prayer
written by the American Theologian Reinhold Niebuhr.
Wikipedia Originally published 1951.)

NEVER!

NEVER!

NEVER GIVE UP!

Section 11

Suggested activities for people who are hurting

Dad and Mom Prayer Group

1 Hour Weekly

<u>Focus</u>
Save Our Children

<u>Mission</u>
Dads and moms uniting in prayer and fasting for
the healing and salvation of their children

<u>Scripture</u>
"Again I say unto you, that if two of you shall agree on earth
as touching anything that they shall ask, it shall be done for
them of my Father which is in heaven. For where two or three
are gathered in my name, there am I in the midst of them."

<u>Matthew 18:19-20 KJV</u>

Where? _____

When? _____

Time: _____

For additional information, contact: _____

Moms Intercessory Prayer Group

Focus: Save Our Sons and Daughters

Mission: Moms coming together to pray God's will for their sons/daughters.

Scripture: "Again I say unto you, that if two of you shall agree on earth as touching anything that they shall ask, it shall be done for them of my Father which is in heaven. For where two or three are gathered in my name, there am I in the midst of them."

Matthew 18:19-20 KJV

Where? _____

When? _____

Time: _____

For additional information, call: _____

Hurting Women Sharing Session

"Together We Can Stand"

<u>Purpose</u>
To bring together hurting women for inspiration,
information, and instruction

<u>The Agenda</u>
Prayer ......Praise and Worship.......The Word

<u>Organizational Structure</u>

- Team Leader.......Schedule the sessions and coordinate
- Prayer Leader......Conducts the Prayer
- Praise and Worship Leader...Conducts Praise and Worship
- The Word.........Select a different speaker for each session

<u>Theme:</u> "Heal me, O Lord and I shall be healed;
Save me and I shall be saved
for thou art my praise!"
<u>Jeremiah 17:14 KJV</u>

<u>Theme Song:</u> "You Won't Leave Here The Way You Came"
(You may select a different song if you wish)

Keep it Simple!

Good Hugging

(To embrace)

People who are hurting need a good hug!

Good hugging is healthy

Good hugging can reduce stress

Good hugging is just like a miracle drug

Good hugging has pleasant effects

Try giving a hug away every day.
(Ask the person "May I give you a hug?)

If the person do not wish to be hugged just tell them "God loves you!"

Hurting Women Outreach

Theme
"We Offer You JESUS"

"Heal me O' Lord and I shall be healed; save me and
I shall be saved; For thou art my praise."
Jeremiah 17:14

Mission Statement
Reaching hurting women in and out of the Body
of Christ with the message of Jesus Christ

Location: _____

Date: _____

Time: _____

Guest Speaker: _____

Contact person:_____@_____

Hurting Women Praise Breakfast

(Spiritual Food Only!)

<u>Theme</u>
"Thus saith the Lord of host, consider ye, call for the mourning women, that they may come; and send for the cunning women that they may come." Jeremiah 9:17

<u>Purpose</u>
Hurting women coming together for inspiration, instruction and information

<u>Theme Song</u>
(You may select a song)

<u>Order of Service</u>

Call to order with scripture and song

Part 1
"Lord Teach Us to Pray"
Prayer Leader in charge

Part 2
Testimonies of answered prayers
(3-5 minutes per person)

Part 3
The Spoken Word
(Select a guest speaker)

Part 4
A Call to pray for persons needing special prayer

Part 5
Announcements and Benediction

Closing Poem

God's Calling for a Woman

Mary A. Brown, M.Ed., D. Min.

There's a woman God's calling for;
In these last and evil days.
A sanctified, dedicated, consecrated laborer;
who will do the things He says.

A woman who will cry aloud and spare not;
Who will lift up her voice loud and bold.
One who will warn the people in this day and time;
In a desperate effort to save men's souls.

God wants a woman who will live a holy life;
So others may know His righteous ways.
He wants a clean and devoted woman;
Who will be an example of the things she says.

God wants a woman who will walk up right;
On Monday, Tuesday, Wednesday and Thursday too.
One who will speak the truth;
On Friday, Saturday, Sunday and the whole week through.

God wants a woman who's not tossed to and fro;
With everything that comes along.
One who will stand up for the right;
When everybody else is going wrong.

God wants a woman whose words are few;
And that's seasoned with grace.
A woman who's willing to pay the price;
In order to win this Christian race.

God wants a praying, a cunning,
a mourning woman too.
He wants a Spirit-filled woman…
Can that woman be *You*?

References

- Names of God, https://bible.org
- Seven Principles of Prayer: https://churchtrainer.com
- Understanding Eight Prayer Watches: https://unitedinchristcanton.org
- Four Types of Fasting: https://www.allaboutprayer.org
- Bible Facts, Wikipedia
- Bible Study Tools: https:www.biblesstudytools.com/bible-versions
- Bible Study Tools:
- https://www.bible-reading.com/bible-plan.html
- List of English Bible Translations-Wikipedia
- Praise: Through Seven Hebrew Words
- Anointed-Word.org
- Bible: www.dictionary.com
- Emotional Distress Signs-https://www.webmd.com
- Dictionary.com
- https://www.google.com

Bibliography

Hemphill, K., *The Names of God*, 1945
Broadman's Holman Publishers
sss

Munroe, M., *In Pursuit of Purpose*, 1992
Destiny Image-Diplomat Press
www.destinyimage.com

Warren, R., *The Purpose Driven Life*, 2002
Zondervan
www.zondervan.com

The End

Printed in the United States
By Bookmasters